ghazni

PROVINCIAL HANDBOOK / A Guide to the People and the Province

Bamyan

Wardak

Uruzgan

Du Abi

Nawur

Shahid
Khogiani

Rashidan

Khwaja
Omari

Zanakhan

Dado

Ajristan

Sangar

Gul
Bahawari

Ghazni

Ramak

Malistan

Jaghatu

Ghazni

Malistan

Waghez

Deh Yak

Qara Bagh

Miray

Andar

Jaghori

Qara Bagh

Sang-e Masha

Pana

Giro

Muqur

Haji
Khel

Muqur

Aab Band

Zabul

Janda

Gelan

Paktika

Nawa

Nawa

Pakistan

Ghazni

———	Roads
▭▭▭	District Border
———	River
⊙	Provincial Center
●	City

LOWER ELEVATION   HIGHER ELEVATION

Table of Contents

List of Tables and Maps

LIST OF TABLES

LIST OF MAPS

Acronyms and Key Terms

ABP	Afghan Border Police
ADT	Agribusiness Development Team
ANA	Afghan National Army
ANBP	Afghan National Border Police
ANDS	Afghan National Development Strategy
ANP	Afghan National Police
ANSF	Afghan National Security Forces
Arbakai	A volunteer, tribal police force which follows a strict ethical code
AWCC	Afghan Wireless Communication Company
BEFA	Basic Education for Afghanistan
BPHS	Basic Package of Health Services
CA	Civil Affairs
CDCs	Community Development Councils
CERP	Commander's Emergency Response Program
CHC	Comprehensive Health Centers
COIN	Counter Insurgency
CSO	Central Statistics Office
DDS	District Development Shuras
DIAG	Disbandment of Illegal Armed Groups
DoS	US Department of State
DST	District Support Team
FATA	Federally Administered Tribal Areas
GIRoA	Government of the Islamic Republic of Afghanistan
HIG or HIH	Hezb-e Islami Gulbuddin ("Islamic Party" formed by Gulbuddin Hekmatyar)

HIK	Hezb-e Islami Khalis ("Islamic Party" formed by Mohammad Yunus Khalis)
ICRC	International Committee of the Red Cross
IDLG	Independent Directorate for Local Governance
IED	Improvised Explosive Devices
IO	International Organization
IRoA	Islamic Republic of Afghanistan
ISAF	International Security Assistance Force
ISI	Inter-Service Intelligence (Pakistan)
Karez	A small underground irrigation system popular in Afghanistan
LGCD	Local Governance and Community Development Program
Meshrano Jirga	Elders' Assembly, upper house of Afghan National Assembly
MRRD	Ministry of Rural Rehabilitation and Development
Mustafiat	Department of Finance
NDS	National Directorate for Security
NGO	Non-Governmental Organization
NSP	National Solidarity Program
NWFP	North West Frontier Province
Pashtunwali	The Pashtuns' pre-Islamic code of conduct
PC	Provincial Council
PDC	Provincial Development Council
PDP	Provincial Development Plan
PRT	Provincial Reconstruction Team
UN	United Nations
UNAMA	United Nations Assistance Mission in Afghanistan
UNOPS	United Nations Office for Project Services
USACE	US Army Corp of Engineers
USAID	US Agency for International Development
USDA	US Department of Agriculture
Wali	Governor
Wolesi Jirga	People's Assembly, lower house of Afghan National Assembly
Woluswal	District Administrator

Guide to the Handbook

This handbook is a concise field guide to Ghazni for internationals deploying to the province. Field personnel have used these guides in Afghanistan since June 2008 to accelerate their orientation process and to serve as a refresher on different aspects of the province during their tour.

Reading this book will provide a basic understanding of the people, places, history, culture, politics, economy, needs, and ideas of Ghazni . Building upon this understanding can help you:

- build rapport and a regular dialogue with local leaders,

- plan and implement pragmatic strategies (security, political, economic) to address sources of instability,

- influence communities to support the political process, not the insurgents, and

- build the capacity and legitimacy of a self-sufficient Afghan government and economy.

SOURCES AND METHODS

These handbooks are not intended as original academic research but as concise, readable summaries for practitioners in the field. The editorial team relies on its collective field experience and knowledge of the province as well as key sources such as the official Islamic Republic of Afghanistan (IRoA), United Nations, and United States Government (USG) publications, and those sources listed in the appendix.

The editors made every effort to ensure accuracy. It should be noted, however, that there is often considerable disagreement regarding what is "ground truth" in Ghazni and things are constantly changing. As such, consider this book part of your orientation, and not an all-inclusive source for everything you need to know.

Information in this handbook is unclassified. The views and opinions expressed in this handbook are those of IDS International and in no way reflect the views of the United States Government or the United States Army.

THE ELECTRONIC UPDATE

Look for electronic updates to this book at *www.idsinternational.net/afpakbooks*. Updates will cover new developments, issues, and leaders that emerge after publication. They will also provide corrections and expanded content in key areas based on input from readers.

We hope the handbook will continue to be a valuable tool in thinking about the challenges in Ghazni. If you have questions, comments, or feedback for future updates or editions please email *afpakbooks@idsinternational.net.*

ABOUT IDS INTERNATIONAL

Publisher of Afghanistan Provincial Handbook Series and the FATA/NWFP Pakistan Books

This book is one of a series of handbooks on Afghanistan provinces and regions of Pakistan. Titles include Ghazni, Helmand, Kandahar, Khost, Kunar, Laghman, Nangarhar, Nuristan, Paktya, and Paktika. Pakistan titles include NWFP and FATA.

In addition to publishing these handbooks, IDS International provides training and analysis to government and private organizations in the areas of politics, economics, culture, stability operations, reconstruction, counterinsurgency, and interagency relations. In particular, IDS is a leading trainer of the US military in working with Provincial Reconstruction Teams (PRTs) in Iraq and Afghanistan. IDS offers its clients expertise and experience in the difficult work of interagency collaboration in complex operations. The writers and editors on this project offer a lifetime of experience working in these provinces and share a dedication to bringing peace and prosperity to the people of Afghanistan.

Author: Paul Fishstein and Gerrard Russell
Editor: Amy Frumin
Assistant Editors: Tom Viehe and Chris Hall

IDS INTERNATIONAL GOVERNMENT SERVICES

1916 Wilson Boulevard

Suite 302

Arlington, VA 22201

703-875-2212

www.idsinternational.net

afpakbooks@idsinternational.net

PUBLISHED: MAY 2010

This and other AfPak handbooks may be purchased in either hard copy or digital format. Samples are available upon request. IDS International is also a leading provider of training and support on the cultural, political, economic, interagency and information aspects of conflict. For inquires, please email *afpakbooks@idsinternational.net* or call 703-875-2212.

More than half of Ghazni's households are involved in agriculture, from growing cereals such as wheat (pictured here) to growing fruits for export.

PHOTO BY BOB MEIER

Chapter 1
Overview and Orientation

ORIENTATION

Ghazni lies at Afghanistan's crossroads. It sits on the fault line that divides its mountainous interior from its southern desert flatlands. This same fault line also divides Ghazni's Pashtun and Hazara ethnic groups, marking the boundary between some of the country's most peaceful and some of its most dangerous areas. In most Pashtun areas of the province, the word of the Taliban rules as law.

Ghazni lies on the main road heading south from Kabul. Trade and supplies moving between Kabul or Kandahar and the southeast provinces must pass through Ghazni. This makes the highway a magnet for the Taliban and criminals.

Ghazni is also home to the Noorulmadaris, one of Afghanistan's most prestigious religious training colleges, from which many of the Taliban's senior leadership graduated.

Districts

Ghazni's approximately one million inhabitants are spread out over almost 9,000 square miles, an area slightly larger than New Jersey. Ninety percent of them live in its roughly 3,100 villages or isolated farmsteads along the rivers that irrigate the province. Most roads are in disrepair, meaning that the people of Ghazni have little access to services.

Ghazni is divided into 19 districts. Located in the province's northeast, Ghazni district is the commercial center and seat of the provincial capital, Ghazni City. It is home to a mixture of ethnicities, including Pashtun, Hazara, and Tajik. While government officials are comfortable travelling safely through the district, the district remains susceptible to insurgent attacks.

Insurgent and criminal activities characterize the districts just north of Ghazni City – Khawja Omari, Shahid Khogiani, and Rashidan. Cars on the roads in Khwaja Omari are subject to frequent attacks by insurgents and criminals. The Afghan Army in Shahid Khogiani was attacked in 2006. In May 2008, Rashidan's district center was briefly captured by the Taliban.

Hazaras constitute a majority in the northwestern districts – including Nawur, Jaghatu, Jaghori, and Malistan. These districts are considered peaceful and secure. Nawur, in the north, is cold and poor. Potable water is scarce and many men work as unskilled laborers. Just west of the Ghazni provincial center, Jaghatu district suffers from high crime, frequent Taliban attacks, and checkpoints along the Kabul-Kandahar highway. Jaghori district is notable for the high levels of education, with 33 schools for boys and girls. However, Hazaras in its southern villages complain of occasional Taliban harassment from the Pashtuns in the neighboring districts. Similarly, the summer influx of Pashtun kuchi nomads through Malistan causes tension with the local Hazara population.

Ajristan, the only Pashtun dominated district in northwestern Ghazni, has a strong Hezb-e Islami and Hezb-e Islami-e Gulbuddin (HIG) presence. It is noteworthy that the Hezb-e Islami was Afghanistan's first revolutionary Islamic movement, appearing in the 1970s, but has since splintered. Presently the term is used to describe two different but closely related movements: one, the registered political party Hezb-e Islami (HI), which is affiliated with the government; the other, the militant insurgent movement Hezb-e Islami-e Gulbuddin (HIG). HI claims to be distinct from HIG and peaceful in orientation. Ajristan was once very dangerous, but since Polish forces conducted operations in summer 2009 it has been considered safe for government and international officials. There are very few schools in the district.

Located in the middle of the province, Qara Bagh district is divided equally between Pashtuns and Hazaras. The Taliban are very active in the Pashtun areas, killing police and intimidating the Pashtun population. In 2007, it had the highest reported sightings of Taliban (37 percent of people saw/heard of them). Nevertheless, government officials have little difficulty traveling safely through the district. Qara Bagh is home to 52 schools but most lack buildings.

Districts along the northeastern border of Ghazni – Zanakhan, Deh Yak, Andar, Giro, and Waghez – are dominated by the Andar, a Pashtun tribe who have often been heavily influenced by the Taliban. Andar district is a Taliban stronghold, where the Taliban killed two people who had promised to bring security to the district. Government officials are wary of visiting much of Andar district for this reason. Roadside bombs and ambushes were a frequent occurrence in Zanakhan throughout 2008. The district's police chief was killed by a roadside bomb in August 2008. In 2007, about 40 percent of Deh Yak inhabitants said they believed Taliban propaganda. Giro's district center was briefly occupied by the Taliban in April 2007 and government officials remain reluctant to visit much of the surrounding district. In mid-2008, Waghez was the site of heavy fighting between Taliban and US forces.

The southeastern districts of Ghazni see little of the provincial government. Gelan was a Taliban stronghold prior to 2001 and today remains dangerous for government officials. The district is infertile and partly desert. The area along the Kabul-Kandahar highway sees frequent criminal activity. Nawa, the southernmost district, was considered so insecure and scarcely populated that no polling centers were opened in the district for the August 2009 presidential election.

Key Towns

While Ghazni City was once one of the most significant cities of Central Asia, repeated destruction and gradual decline have left little evidence of its former greatness. Ghazni City is the former imperial capital of the Ghaznavid Dynasty. At the center of an empire that once stretched from modern-day Iraq to India, Ghazni City was the most important city in South Asia. Today it is the smallest city in Afghanistan; it is Ghazni's provincial capital and the only urban center. As the province's largest city, Ghazni City has roughly 51,000 inhabitants. Remnants of its history are scattered throughout the city – the "Towers of Victory," built in the 12th century as monuments to the victories of the imperial armies, are two minarets located at the bottom of a hill; a 150-foot high citadel built in the 13th century overlooks the city; the tomb of Mahmoud of Ghazni, the Ghaznavid Dynasty's greatest ruler, can be found on the outskirts of the city. During the winter, the city is blanketed by heavy snow due to its high altitude (7,300 feet).

RELEVANT HISTORICAL ISSUES

From Ancient to Modern Times

Ghazni is regarded as the cradle of Afghan culture and arts. During the dynasty of Sultan Mahmoud Ghaznavi, hundreds of scholars and poets flocked to the imperial court, including Ferdowsi, who presented his masterpiece to the sultan – the *Shahnameh*, an epic poem detailing the mythical history of Central Asia. The Ghaznavis' rule lasted for more than two centuries. Since then, Ghazni has been invaded by many empires. Allauddin Ghori, a leader from central Afghanistan, razed Ghazni City to the ground and massacred its population, earning him the nickname *Jahansuz*, or "World Burner." The city was destroyed again by the armies of Genghis Khan in 1221. It was the focus of many campaigns during the Anglo-Afghan wars of the 19th century, changing hands several times.

Communist Era (1979-1992)

The Communists' first leader, Nur Mohammad Taraki, was from Ghazni. Nevertheless, the subsequent mujahedin resistance movement caused Ghaznians to suffer under Communist rule, due mainly to the bloody and eventually successful resistance of the mujahedin (the word means "those who fight in God's cause") to the Communist government.

In the beginning, the mujahedin in Ghazni were dominated by socially conservative but politically moderate factions, especially those linked to Pir Mojaddedi *(see Ch. 3)*. However, funding came easiest to those groups that killed the largest numbers of Soviet troops, and over time this favored the more ruthless and fundamentalist groups which were less dominated by the old feudal aristocracy. By the 1990s the two biggest jihadi movements among Pashtuns in Ghazni were the Hezb-e Islami of Gulbuddin Hekmatyar (HIG) and the Harikat-e Inqilab-e Islami.

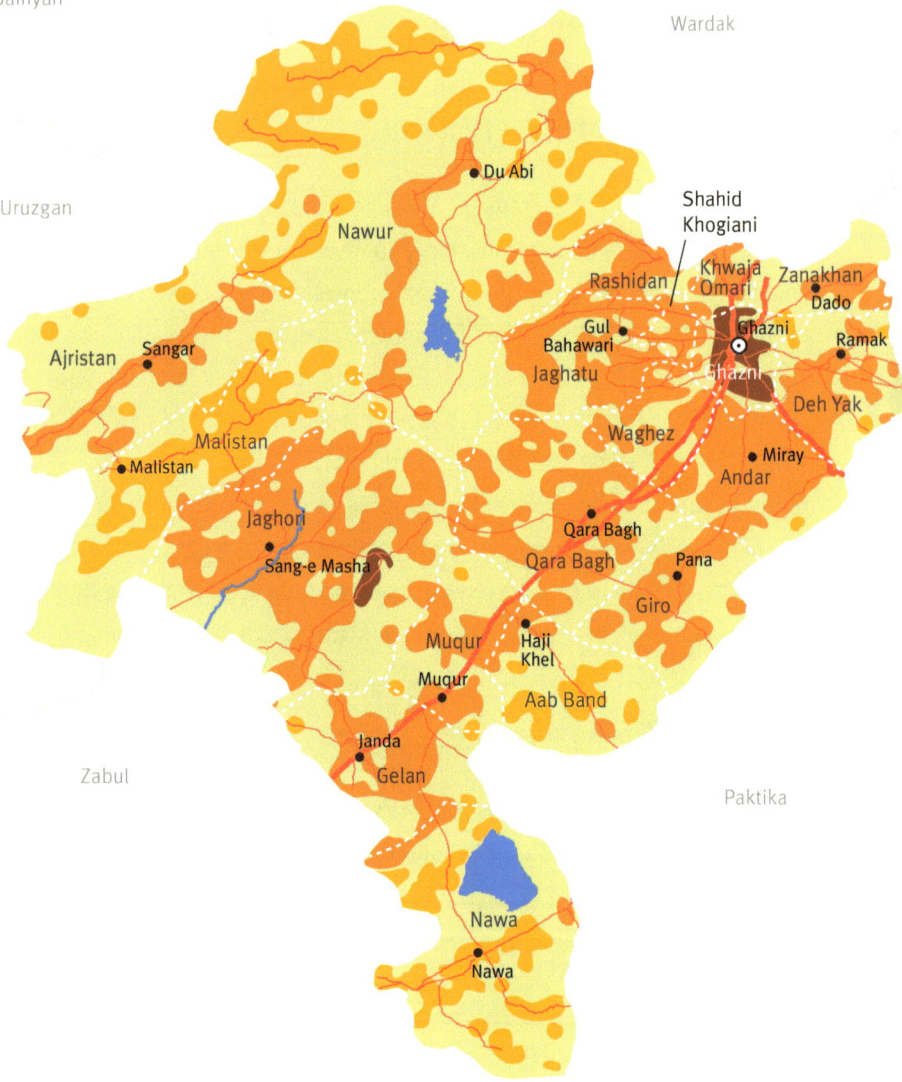

Map 1. Population Map of Ghazni

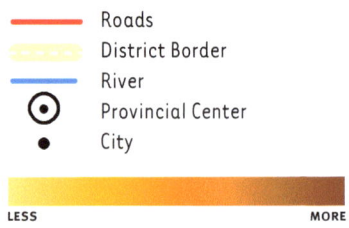

Bamyan

Wardak

Uruzgan

Nawur

Du Abi

Shahid
Khogiani

Rashidan

Khwaja
Omari

Zanakhan

Dado

Ghazni

Ramak

Ajristan

Sangar

Gul
Bahawari
Jaghatu

Deh Yak

Malistan

Waghez

Malistan

Miray
Andar

Jaghori

Sang-e Masha

Qara Bagh

Pana

Qara Bagh

Giro

Muqur

Haji
Khel

Muqur

Aab Band

Zabul

Janda

Gelan

Paktika

Nawa

Nawa

Pakistan

Roads
District Border
River
Provincial Center
City

LESS   MORE

Table 1: District Populations

DISTRICT	CENTER	POPULATION	ETHNICITY (TRIBES)
Provincial Center-Ghazni	Ghazni	154,618	Mixed – Pashtun, Hazara, Tajik, Sikhs, and Hindus
Jaghori	Sang-e Masha	152,162	Hazara
Qara Bagh	Qara Bagh	132,174	Pashtun (Andar), Hazara
Andar	Miray	120,277	Pashtun (Andar)
Nawur	Du Abi	81,909	Hazara (Day Dehqan, Day Mirkasha)
Malistan	Malistan	71,784	Hazara (Day Fawlad)
Gelan	Janda	52,073	Pashtun (Taraki, Mullakhel)
Muqur	Muqur	47,425	Pashtun (Sulimankhel)
Deh Yak	Ramak	44,386	Pashtun (Andar), Tajik
Giro	Pana	38,110	Pashtun (Andar, Taraki)
Waghez	Waghez	36,531	Pashtun (Andar), Hazara
Jaghatu	Gul Bahawari	29,378	Hazara (Qataghan, Day Mirkasha), Pashtun minority
Aab Band	Haji Khel	26,124	Pashtun (Taraki)
Ajristan	Sangar	24,865	Pashtun (Mullakhel)
Zanakhan	Dado	17,518	Pashtun (Andar)
Khwaja Omari	Khwaja Omari	17,475	Mixed – Pashtun, Hazara, Tajik
Shahid Khogiani	Khogiani	16,608	Pashtun (Khogiani)
Rashidan	Rashidan	12,279	Pashtun (mainly Khogiani)
Nawa	Nawa	5,147	Pashtun (Taraki)
TOTAL		**1,080,843**	

Source: Central Statistics Office/UNFPA Socio-Economic and Demographic Profile.

Harikat-e Inqilab-e Islami was later assimilated into the Taliban. Among Hazaras, the jihadi movements that proved most successful were those which had Iranian funding.

Poverty, drought, and the violence of the civil war caused widespread emigration. In the most war-affected areas, as much as 30 percent of the population left the country for Iran or Pakistan. In subsequent years, some of these emigrants have prospered and sent remittances back to their families in Ghazni. These emigrants have also built trade links around family connections in Pakistan.

Ethnic relations continued to be influenced by the patterns and events of the previous 100 years. During the Communist rule, Hazaras initiated clashes at Jaghori and Anguri attempting to reclaim lands which were previously appropriated from them by Pashtun rulers. *(see Ch. 2)*.

Mujahedin and Taliban (1992-2001)

The mujahedin government that replaced the Communist government was unable to establish law and order. Jihadi factions could not agree on a leader and fought among themselves, committing many atrocities against civilians. The Taliban emerged in Kandahar in 1994 initially as a protest movement against mujahedin misrule. Pakistan, seeing the mujahedin government as unfavorable to its interests, gave the Taliban material support. In Pashtun areas, the mujahedin government was unable to stop the advance of the Taliban from Kandahar to Kabul. Along the way, the Taliban quickly enlisted or replaced local mujahedin rulers. Ghazni City fell to the Taliban in January 1995. Non-Pashtun areas resisted the Taliban more fiercely, and in Ghazni the Taliban besieged the Hazara areas rather than assaulting them militarily. As a result, in 1997 food shortages led to widespread hunger in Hazara areas of Ghazni and neighboring provinces.

Contemporary Events (2002-present)

Both Pashtun and Hazara communities were changed forever by the Communist government's attempts to reduce the power of the feudal aristocracy (known as *sardars*, *khans*, and *maliks*). The aristocracy's land was partially redistributed and many left the country. Among Pashtuns in Ghazni, the clergy partly took their place as community leaders and still have a very prominent role today as potential allies or spoilers for the government *(see Ch. 2, Role of Religion)*.

Since 2002, Ghazni has had a series of five governors; the general perception is that most, if not all, have been ineffective. Ghazni's governors have been Asadullah Khalid, 2002-2005; Sher Alam, 2005-2006; Merajuddin Pathan, 2006-2007; Faizanullah Faizan, 2007-2008; Sher Khosti, 2008; and Mohammad Osmani, 2008-present. Only one of these (Faizan) was a native of Ghazni. Security was strongest under Asadullah Khalid; however, he was governor long before the Taliban regained their strength in the province. He is widely criticized for his use of militias, allegedly running private prisons, and engaging in the drug trade.

Under Sher Alam and Merajuddin Pathan, security visibly deteriorated as the Taliban sought to control the outlying districts of the province. The Taliban began an assassination campaign against government officials, killing 28 officials in Andar district in a six month period in 2005-2006. In March 2006, the jihadi leader Qari Baba was murdered after publicly promising to restore security to Andar district.

In the summer of 2007 the Taliban began a murder and intimidation campaign. In normally peaceful Jaghori, the district chief of police's house was attacked and his family killed. In Andar district, four judges were kidnapped and murdered. The Taliban kidnapped 23 Korean Christian missionaries travelling on the Kabul-Kandahar highway.

Ghazni became notorious as a center for Taliban-affiliated kidnap gangs who mainly targeted wealthy Afghans. Ghazni was then used as a launching pad for Taliban infiltration of Wardak province.

Faizanullah Faizan, affiliated with Hezb-e Islami and the first native governor of the province since 2001, reduced the violence through diplomacy and negotiation but was removed after a few months. His successor, Sher Khosti, was naïve and inexperienced. Mohammad Osmani, the current governor, has more experience and is energetic in his political outreach, but has not successfully rolled back Taliban influence. In December 2008, Abdurahim Desiwal, sub-governor of Andar district, was gunned down in Ghazni City. He was reportedly the last sub-governor of one of Ghazni's troubled eastern districts who tried to confront the Taliban.

In the 2009 elections, official figures suggest that Hazaras turned out to vote in far higher numbers than Pashtuns, overwhelmingly choosing the Hazara presidential candidate Ramazan Bashardost. Pashtuns in Ghazni complained of widespread Taliban intimidation and some local radio stations stopped broadcasting news of the election, as well as music and entertainment, after being threatened by the Taliban.

Table 2: Main Jihadi Factions

NAME	LEADER	HOW IT WAS 1980s-1990s	HOW IT IS IN GHAZNI TODAY
Hezb-e Islami-e Gulbuddin (HIG)	Gulbuddin Hekmatyar (in exile)	A Pashtun movement favoring worldwide Islamic revolution. Unlike the Taliban, it favored democracy and female education, and had a strong urban base.	Some of its members have now formed the "Hezb-e Islami" as a peaceful democratic movement which has gained strength in Ghazni; others are insurgents still openly loyal to Hekmatyar. HI members in Ghazni now are pro-Karzai and appear to be peaceful. Their critics allege they are all covertly loyal to Hekmatyar, but many of the government's most competent officials are party members. Khalid Farooqi is the national party leader.
Hezb-e Islami-e Khalis (HIK)	Younis Khalis (deceased)	A splinter faction of the HIG. The two split over issues of leadership and tactics rather than ideology.	Today it is a peaceful movement. The remaining militant members in south-east Afghanistan have joined Haqqani.
Jamiat-e Islami	Burhanudin Rabbani	Mainly based in Northern Afghanistan. The first Islamic resistance movement from which others broke off. Ahmad Shah Masoud was its military commander.	Jamiatis in Ghazni are mainly Tajiks rather than Pashtuns. Jamiat is hostile to the insurgency, but very critical of President Karzai Their candidate in the August 2009 elections was Abdullah Abdullah, who came in second to Karzai.
Harikat-e Inqilab-e Islami	N/A	A Pashtun fundamentalist movement that was essentially rural-based and traditionalist.	Many of its members have now joined the Taliban. Qari Baba (d 2006) was a notable exception.
Mahaz-e Milli	Pir Gailani	A moderate Pashtun religious movement led by Pir Gailani, hereditary leader of a Sufi sect.	Dwindling in importance. It is anti-insurgency, pro-government.
Hezb-e Wahdat	Abdul Ali Mazari (until 1993); Karim Khalili (1993-present)	A Hazara coalition of nine smaller parties. A small anti-Khalili splinter movement broke off and developed ties with the Taliban.	Splinter movements and its failure to deliver benefits post-2001 have weakened its popular base. It remains influential within the Kabul government. Khalili is close to Karzai.
Harikat-e Islami	Ayatollah Mohseni	A Shia movement with support from Iran. Was part of the Hezb-e Wahdat under Khalili, but Mohseni was a powerful figure in his own right.	As with Hezb-e Wahdat, it has lost popular support since 2001. Its leadership supports Karzai, but ordinary members generally do not.

Ghazni's population is divided ethnically, between Pashtun, Hazara, and Tajik, and further divided into tribes and subtribes. Tribal identity is strongest among Pashtuns.

PHOTO BY MICHAEL SMITH

Chapter 2
Ethnicity, Tribes,
Languages and Religion

ETHNICITY

The ethnic composition of the province as a whole is estimated to
be 50 percent Pashtun, 44 percent Hazara, and six percent Tajik.
Individual districts tend to be concentrated with one group. Even
where districts are mixed, ethnic groups tend to be separated (e.g.,
Jaghori). Ghazni City is home to Tajiks and a very small number of
Sikhs and Hindus. These communities originally came to Ghazni for
its commercial opportunities and have lived there for generations.
In addition, there are pockets of small communities of Turkic origin
living in Ghazni. Generally, Hazaras live towards the northwest and
Pashtuns towards the southeast. Pockets of Pashtu speakers live in
the northwest and kuchis move through some of the northwestern
districts in search of better pastures in the summer.

Table 3: Major Tribes in Ghazni

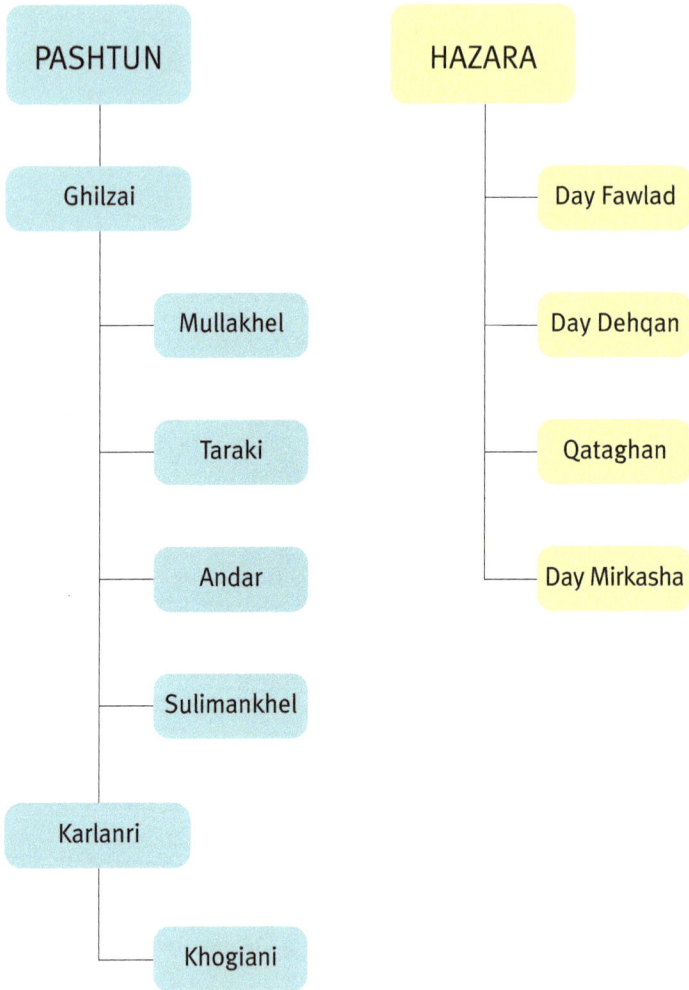

PASHTUN
- Ghilzai
  - Mullakhel
  - Taraki
  - Andar
  - Sulimankhel
- Karlanri
  - Khogiani

HAZARA
- Day Fawlad
- Day Dehqan
- Qataghan
- Day Mirkasha

Hazaras

Hazaras, most of whom practice Shia Islam, are thought to be descended from Ghengis Khan's Mongol armies. They have traditionally been discriminated against by Pashtun-dominated governments in Kabul. Placed at the bottom of the socio-economic ladder, they worked largely as servants and laborers and, until the early 20th century, as slaves. They still form a large part of the unskilled labor market in Kabul, but through education, greater access to government jobs, and commercial ties with Hazaras in Pakistan and Iran, they are slowly improving their socio-economic standing. Hazaras are much more open to education for boys and girls as a route to future betterment. This openness is most evident in Jaghori district, which has 33 high schools.

Their relationship with the Pashtuns has been strained since the 1880s, when Amir Abdurahman carried out a military program to subdue the previously autonomous Hazaras and bring them under the control of the growing Afghan state. From 1992-1996, Pashtun and Hazara jihadi factions brutally fought each other, creating lasting resentments. Hazaras generally believe that their homeland, a mountainous region in central Afghanistan known as Hazarajat, was intentionally divided among ten provinces, including Ghazni, in order to dilute Hazaras' political strength. Likewise, districts in Ghazni have been divided in the past twenty years in ways that generally favor Pashtuns.

Hazaras broadly support the government and NATO against the Taliban. Nevertheless, many believe the government is ineffective and ethnically biased against them. This perception led the Hazara population to vote en masse for firebrand leftist Ramazan Bashardost in the August 2009 elections.

Pashtuns

Pashtuns are an Indo-European ethnic group that is subdivided into tribes and clans. They have a strong sense of tribal identity. Traditionally tribes made decisions as a group and often were ruled by hereditary khans and maliks. Tribal solidarity is less entrenched in Ghazni than in the provinces of Loya Paktya to the southeast (modern day Paktya, Paktika, and Khost). Instead, the clergy have become more influential than the traditional tribal leaders.

Pashtuns have historically been the dominant ethnic group in Afghanistan and some of them feel resentment at the power now held by Tajiks and Hazaras in the government in Kabul. Tension between Pashtuns and Hazaras has existed for centuries. The two groups are ethnically quite distinct, and practice different versions of Islam *(see "Role of Religion" below)*. Both groups claim grievances against the other. Hazaras claim that Pashtuns settled on their land in areas like Ajristan, while Pashtuns claim that this land was originally theirs before the invasion of Genghis Khan. These grievances and the religious differences between the two groups did not lead to violence until Afghanistan's vicious civil war of 1992-1996, nor have they since, but they help to explain why the two communities tend to live separately, and why the Taliban has sought and found few allies among the Hazaras. The insurgency in Afghanistan is carried out almost exclusively by Pashtuns.

Pashtuns in Afghanistan, including Ghazni, are geographically close to Pakistan, and share a common culture and language with Pashtun tribes on the other side of the border. As a consequence, cultural and commercial ties between cross-border tribes are strong. Indeed, many Afghan clergy are trained in Pakistani madrassas, which can be a significant asset for the Taliban as many of these madrassas are sympathetic to the Taliban theology.

Kuchis

Traditionally, large parts of Afghanistan were inhabited by nomads on a seasonal basis because much of the land was not fertile enough to sustain a settled population year-round. As the summer approached, nomads would move their sheep, goats, and camels towards higher pastures where snow had recently melted and the grass was greener. Today this way of life is still in practice on a smaller scale by the *kuchis*, a mainly Pashtun group of the Ahmadzai, Sulimanzai, and other tribes. Some members of these tribes have bought land and settled down but still call themselves kuchis. There are an estimated three million kuchis in Afghanistan; they have ten seats reserved for them in the lower house of Parliament because they are not residents of specific provinces.

In Ghazni, the kuchis are all Pashtun. In winter they number around 30,000 and in summer over 120,000. Their summer migration has taken them, for most of the past hundred years, up through the higher-altitude land inhabited by Hazaras. The Hazaras dispute these rights and at times have managed to prevent this migration by force (as they did during the 1980s). While conflicts between the settled Hazaras and the nomadic kuchi occur almost annually, they rarely lead to bloodshed. The most serious recent flare-up was in Wardak province (north of Ghazni) in 2008 when armed warfare broke out between the two groups, resulting in a number of deaths and the destruction of whole villages. The government has tried to negotiate between the two groups and succeeded in averting conflict in 2009 by paying a large sum of money to kuchi leaders. Although the potential for conflict is greatest in Wardak province, tensions have also flared up in parts of Ghazni (in Jaghori and Malistan districts in particular). The Hazaras accuse the kuchis of having links with the Taliban, and indeed they were favored by the Taliban government. However, it is unclear where their present allegiance lies.

Other Ethnicities

Ghazni has a wide variety of smaller ethnic groups which include Tajiks, Sikhs, and Hindus (descendants of traders and others that came to Afghanistan by migration in the past two hundred years), and descendants of Turk/Azeri communities (the Bayat and the Chagatai).

TRIBES AND CLANS

While Ghazni's population is divided among Pashtun, Hazara, and Tajik, each is further divided into tribes and sub-tribes. Pashtun society is divided into two main groups – **Durrani,** who were politically dominant and included the royal family; and **Ghilzai.** Each of these "super-tribes" is further divided into tribes. The main Pashtun tribes in Ghazni are mostly Ghilzai, comprising the **Andar, Sulimankhel, Taraki,** and **Mullakhel.** There are several smaller tribes mostly in the north of the province, the largest of them being the **Khogiani** of the **Karlanri** "super-tribe."

The **Sulimankhel** is a large and diverse tribe, which is spread across east and southeast Afghanistan. Its historical rivals are the Kharoti who, like the Sulimankhel, are more numerous in Paktika. The tribe is represented in both the Afghan government and the senior ranks of the Taliban. The further south the Sulimankhel live, the more pro-Taliban they appear to be. Sulimankhel areas in Ghazni, like those of the Taraki tribe, are somewhat more open to government influence than those of the Andar tribe.

The **Andar** in its eastern districts is heavily under Taliban influence and specifically the influence of the Haqqani Network. Andar tribesmen are famous for the extent and complexity of their *karezes*, the Afghan system of underground irrigation. Although it is a conservative Sunni tribe, the Andar aligned itself for a time with the Shia Harakat-e Islami during the anti-Soviet campaign.

The **Taraki** tribe (in the southern tip of the province) previously supported the Taliban regime but is now somewhat less radicalized than the Andar. Their most famous member was Nur Mohammad Taraki, president of Afghanistan during the Communist government from April 1978 until September 1979.

The **Mullakhel** live in the remote northwest of the province and are cut off from other Pashtun tribes. The Taliban infiltration into their district tends to be from Zabul province to the west. The Mullakhel are strong supporters of Hezb-e Islami, but are less supportive of the Taliban.

Tribal sentiment is not as strong among Hazara, many of whom may not even know what clan they are from. The major Hazara clans (subclans) are **Day Dehqan**, **Day Mirkasha**, **Day Fawlad**, and **Qataghan**.

While tribal areas can be represented on Map 2, the boundaries and separation of the different groups are approximations and there is overlap in many areas, although less so within one settlement or village.

LANGUAGE

Language in Ghazni province follows ethnic patterns: Pashtuns largely speak Pashto, while Hazara and Tajiks speak Dari. In Ghazni City, most people speak Dari both because it is largely the working language of the government and because of greater contact with predominantly Dari-speaking Kabul. Hazaras, especially those from rural areas, speak a dialect of Dari called Hazaragi, which some consider a separate language. It is quite intelligible to Dari speakers despite the unique accent and some differences in vocabulary.

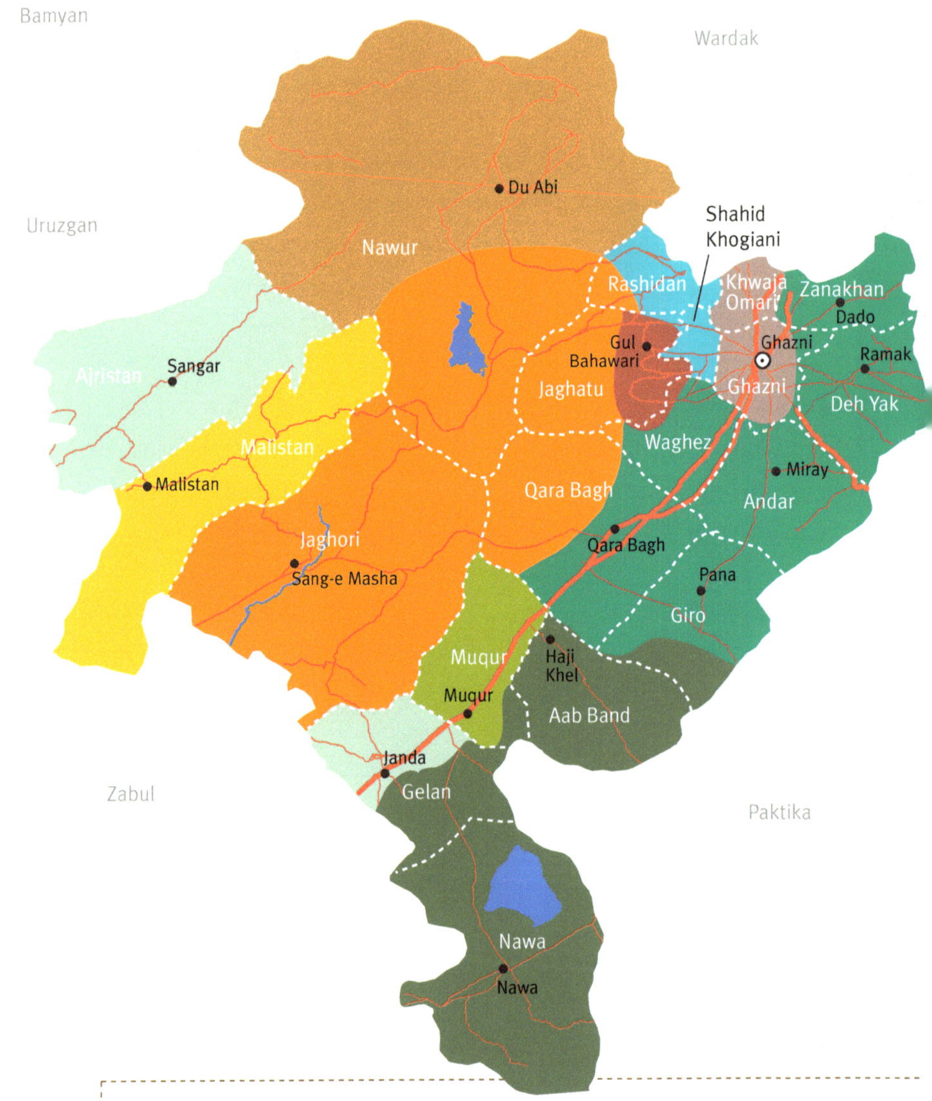

Map 2. Tribal Map of Ghazni

Bamyan

Wardak

Uruzgan

Du Abi

Nawur

Shahid
Khogiani

Rashidan

Khwaja
Omari

Zanakhan

Dado

Ghazni

Ghazni

Ramak

Ajristan

Sangar

Gul
Bahawari

Jaghatu

Waghez

Deh Yak

Malistan

Qara Bagh

Miray

Andar

Malistan

Jaghori

Sang-e Masha

Qara Bagh

Pana

Giro

Muqur

Haji
Khel

Muqur

Aab Band

Janda

Gelan

Zabul

Paktika

Nawa

Nawa

Pakistan

Legend:

- Roads
- District Border
- River
- ⊙ Provincial Center
- • City

GHILZAI PASHTUN
- Mullakhel
- Taraki
- Andar
- Sulimankhel

KARLANRI PASHTUN
- Khogiani

HAZARA
- Day Fawlad
- Day Dehqan
- Qataghan
- Day Mirkasha

- Mixed Tribes

ROLE OF RELIGION

In Afghanistan, religion is a key part of personal identity and is the most important factor in guiding social life. Throughout Afghan history, religion has played a role in motivating (and manipulating) the people to support or oppose the state and other groups. Perceived threats to religion and traditional way of life have led to revolt and civil unrest. At the same time, it is often difficult to separate the influence of religion from that of cultural traditions. For instance, Afghans will sometimes attribute to Sharia (religious law) what is actually local tradition with no theological basis in Islam.

Sunni Islam

Pashtuns are almost all Sunni, like the majority of Muslims worldwide. Sunnis have no clearly defined formal religious hierarchy. Often, the secular ruler would also claim religious authority over his subjects. Today, however, figures like the Imam of the Kaaba (a senior Saudi religious scholar) or the Al-Azhar University in Egypt are widely influential.

Sunni mullahs lead prayers and give basic religious education. Some have been educated at madrassas, almost always in Pakistan. However, Ghazni has one of Afghanistan's few madrassas, the Noorulmadaris. Most Sunni mosques in Ghazni are affiliated with the Taliban, Hezb-e Islami, or Jamiat-e Islami.

Strict practice of religion for Sunni Muslims means praying five times a day, making the Hajj pilgrimage to Islam's holy sites in Saudi Arabia once in a lifetime, avoiding pork and alcohol, donating to charity (often religious charities), and fasting in daylight hours during the month of Ramadan. Conservative Pashtun men do not even like to be asked about female members of their families.

Sufi Islam

Sunnis who particularly revere a specific *pir* (spiritual guide) are Sufis. The two Sufi movements in Afghanistan are the Qadiriyah and the Naqshbandiyah. The pir is a hereditary position. In Afghanistan a member of the Gailani family is pir of the Qadiriyah, and the Mojaddedi family leads the Naqshbandiyah. Both movements are present in Ghazni province, although the number of Sufis has declined in the past thirty years. These Sufi pirs are political moderates and Sufi movements are not linked with the insurgency.

Shia Islam

Shia Muslims, almost all of whom are Hazara in Ghazni, have a formal hierarchy with the Grand Ayatollahs at the top. Grand Ayatollahs are selected for their piety and learning; most are in Najaf, Iraq. An individual Shiite can choose one of these most senior religious figures as his or her *marja*, or spiritual reference; he or she then accepts all the religious judgments of the marja, which may have political significance as well. The remoteness of Afghanistan's Shia means they are more disconnected from this hierarchy than Shia living elsewhere. One of Shia Islam's most senior religious figures, Ishaq Fayadh, is Hazara but he lives in Iraq. Ayatollah Mohseni, a Kabul-based Afghan, has significant influence as a political and religious figure, but he is not Hazara. Secular jihadi leaders and politicians have more leverage with the general Shia population.

Just as Saudi Arabia and Pakistan have influence among Sunni Pashtuns, Iran seeks to extend its influence among the Shia through funding education and other initiatives. Hazaras often have cultural links to Iran because so many of them have spent time there as refugees or economic migrants. There is no natural affection, though, especially as they often suffered racial discrimination while living there. The jihadi leadership cultivates close ties with Iran but the average Hazara does not.

Shia are allowed to combine some of their prayers so that they pray three, rather than five, times a day. They break their fast in Ramadan a little later than Sunnis. They sometimes have their fasts and festivals a day sooner or later than Sunnis. They have an annual day of mourning called Ashura when official business is generally suspended. In Afghanistan, Shia are generally more open to the idea of women going to school and having jobs. They sometimes display pictures of holy men, particularly the Prophet's grandson Hussein. There are other minor differences between Shia and Sunnis, but they are less important for a non-Muslim to know.

Ghaznians line up in front of a polling station during the 2009 presidential election. During the elections, Hazaras voted in greater numbers than Pashtuns, who complained of Taliban intimidation.

PHOTO BY MICHAEL SMITH

Chapter 3
Government and Leadership

The Afghan government suffers from a shortage of talented officials. Most of these prefer positions in Kabul or in richer and safer places like Herat or Nangarhar. However, the government structure requires there to be civilian and security officials at the district level in every province. Sometimes these officials are native to the district and use their positions to establish themselves as powerful local figures. Other times they may be serving out their posts while hoping to move somewhere better. Although provincial and district governors are often regarded by internationals and Afghans as the leading figures in the area, the Constitution in fact limits their authority and funds almost to the point of making them mere figureheads. They therefore have to develop their authority; it is not given to them automatically. Some are good at this, but many are weak or do not care.

HOW THE GOVERNMENT OFFICIALLY WORK

Central Control

The Afghan Constitution concentrates authority and power in the national government, a decision that was taken in order to counter the power of warlords in the provinces. As a result, the provincial government has very little autonomy. Instead, decisions on everything from policy to funding priorities are made in Kabul.

Parliament

The Afghan National Assembly is composed of two houses: the upper house is the Elders' Assembly (*Meshrano Jirga*), and the lower house is the People's Assembly (*Wolesi Jirga*). The Wolesi Jirga has 249 directly-elected delegates (elected by popular vote) including reserved slots for women and nomadic kuchis. The Meshrano Jirga has 102 delegates, one-third elected by Provincial Councils, one-third by District Councils, and one-third appointed by the president. The National Assembly passes laws and the government's budget, questions government ministers, and approves government ministers before they take up their positions. Ghazni has 11 elected representatives in the Wolesi Jirga and two senators in the Meshrano Jirga; three appointed senators are also from Ghazni.

Provincial Government

A governor (*wali*) heads the provincial government and is appointed by and reports to the Independent Directorate for Local Governance (IDLG), located in the Executive Office of the President. He is assisted by a deputy and several staff who oversee provincial government management. The governor is given a small budget to run his office.

The 25 ministries in Kabul execute their policies and programs through departments located at the provincial level. Ministers, with the approval of the president, appoint provincial directors who manage the departments. The director reports to and receives funds from the ministry in Kabul. The governor is not in the chain of command for the directors nor does he have budgetary authority over any of these departments, but must approve all expenditures before they are processed by the Department of Finance (*Mustafiat*).

Provincial Council

The 19-member Provincial Council (PC) is the only elected body at the provincial level. It provides a voice for the people in advising on provincial issues. Its relevance is largely dependent on the governor's support and on its members' individual resources and initiatives. However, a 2007 change to the Afghan Constitution gave the PC the responsibility of approving the Provincial Development Plans (PDP). This new authority gives the PC the ability to be somewhat responsive to its constituency. In Ghazni, five PC seats are reserved for women.

In the 2009 elections, only four members of the previous PC were re-elected. The results, however, are still subject to challenge as there was evidence of widespread fraud.

District and Local Governance

Government at the district level mirrors the provincial government with the *woluswal* (district administrator or sub-governor), Police Chief, National Directorate of Security Officer, clerks, and a small police force. Ministry sub-departments also operate at the district level, but are not present in every district.

District council elections are expected in 2010. In 2007, District Development Assemblies (DDA) were formed in order to plan, prioritize, and coordinate development activities at the district level. The DDA's input goes into the Provincial Development Plan (PDP), which is later incorporated into the final version of the Afghan National Development Strategy (ANDS).

Below the district level, the National Solidarity Program (NSP) has established Community Development Councils (CDCs). NSP is implemented nationally through the Ministry of Rural Rehabilitation and

Development (MRRD), originally with World Bank funding. It seeks to develop the ability of local communities to identify, plan, manage, and monitor their own development projects. The CDCs prioritize, implement, and supervise village level projects. NSP claims representatives of CDCs are "elected;" however, this never genuinely means canvassing the entire population. In some instances, representatives may be "elected" by the simple absence of any objections within the community.

The municipality of Ghazni City is led by a mayor who is appointed by the president in consultation with the governor. Municipalities are independent from the provincial government, are free to plan, fund, and implement projects, and can tax local businesses (a power that Provincial Councils do not have). In practice, the mayor works closely with the governor and the PRT to conduct city planning and projects. The mayor and municipality council are meant to be subject to election, but these elections have not yet taken place.

Provincial Coordination

The Provincial Development Committee (PDC) is formally composed of provincial line directors and the chairman of the Provincial Council. It is chaired by the governor, who can invite members of the international community and the NGO community as non-voting members to ensure coordination among the various development actors active in the province. The Director of Economy acts as the secretariat of the PDC. Participants often include the PRT, USAID, and NGOs. Ideally, Technical Working Groups (TWGs) are established by sector (in accordance with the sectors established in the Afghan National Development Strategy) and chaired by the appropriate line department. The TWGs can report their findings and recommendations at the monthly PDC meeting. The Ghazni PDC was formed in mid-2006, but meets without the full participation of NGOs and UN agencies.

HOW IT ACTUALLY WORKS

Provincial governance is weak and ineffective. Relations between the governor and the PC have deteriorated. PC members accuse Governor Osmani of ignoring their advice, having involvement in the drug trade, and threatening them with violence. As a result, many PC members spent 2009 in Kabul boycotting meetings in protest of the governor's behavior.

Overall, district and provincial governments have been unable to provide services or respond to public needs. The capacity of these institutions is hindered by a shortage of human and financial resources and a lack of consistent supervision, oversight, and motivation. As a result, government officials are inefficient and often embezzle resources and benefits intended to assist the local population. Improving public administration is a constant battle, hindered by a lack of basic skills, willful corruption, ethnic divisions, and poorly-defined programs and objectives. Locals have become alienated by the local government's disinterest, inability, and corruption; as a result, they are grudgingly supporting government opposition such as the Taliban.

Pashtun areas in the province's eastern districts are dominated by the Taliban. Government officials cut deals with the Taliban to guarantee their survival. Locals request Taliban consent before undertaking any major initiatives. The Taliban dissuade provincial radio stations from broadcasting music. The Taliban are more powerful than the government in Pashtun areas of Ghazni. In the August 2009 elections, according to residents of the eastern districts of Ghazni, the Taliban were able to ensure a very low turnout. At their order, families recalled relatives in Kabul back to Ghazni so that they would not vote outside the province. Hazaras in the province's western districts are mostly free from Taliban intimidation. Those living closest to Pashtun areas, however, sometimes complain of Taliban threats.

Ghazni is represented in the Wolesi Jirga by 11 representatives (eight male, three female). Six of the eleven representatives are ex-jihadis, while ethnically the division is six Pashtuns and five Hazaras. During both the 2004 presidential and 2005 parliamentary elections, political campaigning was higher than elsewhere in the region, perhaps due to higher education levels or to greater ethnic diversity.

A new Provincial Council (PC) was elected in August 2009, but the results are subject to challenge and potential re-counts. Prior to the 2009 elections, the 19 member PC was made up of 14 males and five females, and was divided mainly along ethnic lines. While making up less than half the population, Hazaras formed the majority (10) in the PC. The PC suffered from the same constraints as most other provincial bodies: lack of clarity on its role and its authority, low skill levels, and no financial resources.

SECURITY FORCES

The main contingent of international forces in Ghazni is Polish, numbering 1,600 troops in the province. There are also 1,000 American troops and an American PRT.

Coordination among the various security institutions in Ghazni is poor. Locals increasingly see the Afghan army as an effective force, while the police are perceived less positively. The Disarmament, Demobilization, and Reintegration (DDR) Program operated in Ghazni for one year and disarmed roughly 650 people. However, the DDR and subsequent Disbandment of Illegal Armed Groups (DIAG) programs produced mixed success. Several commanders, including some allies of the government and several corrupt police chiefs, still maintain armed militias which prey on the local population.

Afghan National Army (ANA)

The most senior ANA officer is General Rajab Ali Rashid, commander of the third brigade of the 203rd military corps. The corps is headquartered in Gardez and commanded by Major General Abdul Khaliq. The third brigade has its full complement of 588 soldiers, who currently operate in Ghazni City, Muqur, Andar, Rashidan, and along the Kabul-Ghazni Highway.

National Directorate of Security (NDS)

The NDS, the Afghan intelligence service, has become more effective in Ghazni under the provincial leadership of Dr. Shah Jan, a Hazara, and his deputy General Samar, a Pashtun. Both leaders are widely respected in the province. NDS willingly partners with international security forces but has a shortage of professional and well-trained staff, facilities, and equipment. NDS is viewed with some suspicion across the country and in Ghazni because many of its employees are Tajiks who were trained by and worked for the Communist intelligence agency. More recently, employees have been drawn from the jihadi factions. These different backgrounds, as well as varying ethnic and political allegiances, can undermine its unity of effort. Nevertheless, NDS is generally regarded as the most effective of the state security institutions.

Afghan National Police (ANP)

Like the NDS, the ANP lacks professional and well-trained staff, facilities, and equipment. Officially, the ANP employs 2,412 police, but only 2,000 are paid. Local sources suggest that the real number of police is much less, maybe around 1,200 police. Most police are now paid through a new system that deposits salaries directly into their bank accounts. Insecurity and low pay makes retention difficult.

The ANP suffers from weak leadership and low morale. In Ghazni, locals complain about the behavior and attitude of the police, particularly in insecure districts and at check points. Allegations against the police include taking bribes, using drugs, behaving disrespectfully, or detaining and sexually abusing small boys and girls. In November 2006 police were accused by a local PC member of looting shops in Andar. Pashtuns complain that non-Pashtuns are over-represented in the local police; the lack of official figures detailing the ethnic breakdown of the police makes it impossible to confirm or deny these allegations. Across Afghanistan, ethnic Tajiks tend to dominate the officer class of the police.

Many ANP have been killed recently in Ghazni. In January 2008, a district police chief and eight other police personnel were killed by international military air and ground forces who apparently mistook them for insurgents or criminals. Some attribute the high death rate to the use of the ANP as a counter-insurgency force when it is neither prepared nor equipped to take on the brunt of the counter-insurgency fight. The casualty rate appeared to decrease in 2009, however, down from 120 killed in action (KIA) in 2008 to 20 KIA in the first five months of 2009.

The Afghan National Auxiliary Police (ANAP) was introduced early on in Ghazni, with most of the personnel being sent to insurgent areas. It has now been dissolved and its members have become members of the ANP.

POLITICAL PARTIES

Most of the jihadi factions from Table 2 have transformed into political parties. The table below records other parties that have become significant in Ghazni since 2001.

Table 4: Political Parties

PARTY	DESCRIPTION	LEADER
Eqtedar-e Milli-e Afghanistan	A Hazara party that supported Abdullah Abdullah in August 2009 election.	Ali Kazemi
Hezb-e Wahdat-e Mardum Islami	A Hazara breakaway group from Khalili's Hezb-e Wahdat; it now is pro-Karzai.	Mohammad Mohaqqeq
Afghan Millat	A Pashtun secular nationalist party.	Anwar-ul-Haq Ahadi
Nuzhat-e Hambastagi-e Milli-Afghanistan	A moderate Pashtun party based around a branch of the Gailani family.	Sayed (Pir) Ishaq Gailani
Itihad-e Islami-e Afghanistan	A Pashtun Islamist party that is pro-Karzai.	Abdel-Rabb Sayyaf
Hezb Hambastagi-Mili-Jawanan	A pro-Karzai political party for young people that runs sports and cultural events.	Mohammed Jamil Karzai (President Karzai's second cousin)
Congra-e Milli	A liberal Tajik separatist party.	Abdellatif Pedram

LEADER PROFILES

Government and Political Leaders

Mohammad Osman Osmani, Governor: Appointed in May 2008, Governor Osmani is an Alokazai Pashtun from Kandahar province and a doctor by profession. He was born in 1968 in Dand district of Kandahar. He was educated in Dand district initially and later in Kandahar City. During the Soviet invasion and Communist regime, his family took refuge in Quetta, Pakistan. He actively participated in the jihad as part of a group led by Mullah Naqib, an Alokazai elder and prominent Jamiat-e Islami commander who died in 2007. Three of Osmani's brothers were killed fighting in the jihad; his elder brother Mullah Khudaidad survived and worked as an adviser to the Taliban Defense

Minister. Mullah Khodaidad remains an influential figure in the Alokazai tribe, and now is a member of the Alokazai shura in Kandahar.

Governor Osmani claims to have graduated from Kandahar University in 1999, but some accounts dispute this claim, reporting that he only received basic medical training while working in Pakistan with the ICRC as a medical volunteer for more than 18 years. Before his appointment as governor, he worked as a doctor in Kandahar's provincial hospital and ran his own private clinic. He also served as an influential figure in Kandahar, belonging to several local jirgas and associations of an intellectual, moderate, and progressive bent.

Governor Osmani is supportive of President Karzai and is not affiliated with any other specific political party or group. Before the recent election he was accused of having guaranteed a victory for Karzai in the province (in the end, this did not happen). PC members also accused him of threatening them with violence and being involved in drug smuggling. Prior to this dispute with the PC, Governor Osmani had not been accused of human rights abuses or criminality.

Osmani believes that the Polish military takeover of responsibility for Ghazni has caused security to deteriorate. He personally is politically active in the province and keeps a wide range of contacts, but he has not brought any improvement in security and has many critics.

Haji Mohammad Kazem Allahyar, Deputy Governor: Appointed in July 2005, Allahyar is a Hazara from a well-connected jihadi family based in Ghazni City. (" Haji" is an honorific given to those who have made the pilgrimage to Mecca.) He was briefly deputy governor in 2002, but was soon removed because of poor relations with the then-Governor Asadullah Khalid. In late 2005, he helped a previous Pashtun governor mediate between Hazara and Pashtun groups in the Provincial Council. In May 2006, he was the target of a failed assassination attempt. He has a business importing oil and other goods from Iran. He, along with a group of provincial officials (including

Ghazni's Mayor Hakeemullah Ghazni, the head of finance department Fida Mohammad Azizi, and the head of power and water Jan Mohammad), is accused by local sources of corruption.

Dr. Shah Jan, Head of NDS: A Hazara with good Pashtun connections from Jaghatu district of Ghazni province, Dr. Jan is in his early fifties and a graduate of the medical faculty of Jalalabad University. During the jihad era, he remained with the Harikat-e Islami party led by Ayatollah Mohseni. During the Taliban era, he migrated to the US. After the Taliban regime collapsed, he returned to Afghanistan and worked as an advisor in NDS headquarters. His present political affiliation is with the same Harakat-e Islami party, led by Mohammad Ali Javid.

General Khial Baz Sherzai, Chief of Police: Appointed on 2 April 2009, he is a Zazi Pashtun from Khost province. He was educated in his native village of Ata Khail, at the military school and university in Kabul, and then four years at military college in Moscow. After completing his training, he worked in the Afghan Police and then the Afghan Army. During the Taliban era, he remained at home and took no active part in public life. After the fall of the Taliban he became head of Division 25, a militia force mainly made up of former Communists. This division was responsible for security in Khost after the fall of the Taliban and was later decommissioned. In 2007, Mr. Sherzai became Chief of Police of Farah province.

Dr. Zia Gul, Provincial Health Director: Dr. Gul has served as the Provincial Health Director since 2003. She is the only female Provincial Health Director in Afghanistan. She is from Ghazni City, where her husband is the head of the Ghazni civil hospital.

Other Influential Ghazni Personalities

Daoud Sultanzoy, Wolesi Jirga member: Sultanzoy is Chairman of the Economic Committee of the Wolesi Jirga, which examines legislation that has economic consequences (not including the annual state budget).

A civil pilot by training, after the Soviet invasion of Afghanistan he defected on a plane to Germany. He then worked for foreign airline companies and settled in Southern California. After the fall of the Taliban regime, he returned to Afghanistan and began engaging in political life. He is fluent in English. He supports the Coalition but is an outspoken critic of President Karzai.

Mahmoud Gailani, Wolesi Jira member: Mr. Gailani was born into the well-respected Gailani family in 1978. He helped negotiate the release of South Korean hostages from the Taliban in 2007 and has been described as a prospective top politician of the future. The Gailani family has lost some popularity, however, because they have not delivered enough benefits to their supporters.

Abdul Baqi Baryal, Meshrano Jirga member: Baryal was born in Ajristan district and became a poet and journalist in the 1980s. He lost both his eyes in 1982 in a mine explosion. In 2002, he participated in the Emergency Loya Jirga. He was appointed to the Meshrano Jirga by the President. He is married and has five children.

Ali Ahmad Jalali, national politician: Born in Jaghatu in 1940, Jalali was a colonel in the Afghan army and then, as a refugee in the US, became a presenter on Voice of America. He became a US citizen in 1987. He returned to Afghanistan in 2003 as Interior Minister but then resigned in 2005. He was regarded by Ministry staff as clean but somewhat weak; nonetheless, he was a popular prospective candidate for the Presidency in 2009, although he eventually decided not to run.

Dr. Sima Samar, Head of Afghanistan Independent Human Rights Commission (AIHRC): Born in Jaghori in 1957, she was originally a medical doctor and worked in Jaghori during the Communist era until she was forced to flee to Pakistan in 1984. There she founded and directed the Shuhada Organization, an NGO focused on the welfare of women and children. She returned in 2002 to become Deputy President and then Minister of Women's

Affairs. She was forced from office by fundamentalist Islamic protesters after she had appeared to question some aspects of Islamic law in a newspaper interview. Soon after, she became head of the AIHRC.

Ramazan Bashardost, national politician: Bashardost was a candidate for the presidency in 2009 and won over 10 percent of the vote, including 61 percent of the vote in Ghazni (almost entirely from Hazara voters). He was born in Qara Bagh district in 1965, and left Afghanistan in 1983. He spent some time studying law in Paris and returned to Afghanistan in 2002. He worked in the Ministry of Foreign Affairs and later became the Planning Minister (a position that no longer exists). After leaving his post as Planning Minister, Bashardost was elected to the Wolesi Jirga. He is widely respected by Hazaras and became famous for his campaign against corruption. He practices a life of strict austerity, living in a tent opposite Parliament where he receives large numbers of delegations from across the country. During his presidential campaign he travelled across Afghanistan in a second-hand bus.

Militia, Business, and Religious Leaders

Other significant commanders during the jihad against the Soviets were **Bashi Habib**, a Hezb-e Islami Gulbuddin (HIG) commander from Jaghori, who is now district governor (*woleswal*) of Qara Bagh; and **Khodaidad Erfani**, connected with the Hezb-e Wahdat and now the *woleswal* of Jaghori.

Some of Ghazni's business leaders split their time between Ghazni and Quetta, including **Haji Ali Nawroz** and **Haji Jan Ali**, both of whom are Hazara. Business tends to be import/export, with an emphasis on import, as Ghazni has almost no manufacturing base.

Khalifa Jan Mohammad runs the important theological college the Noorulmadaris Madrassa. This madrassa is significant as it was attended by a number of senior Taliban figures, and because it is one of very few in Afghanistan.

Ghazni's economy is primarily agricultural, but Ghazni City's location on the Kabul-Kandahar highway and its proximity to the Pakistani border have allowed this area to prosper as a market town.

PHOTO BY MICHAEL SMITH

Chapter 4
The Economy

G hazni's standard of living is average for Afghanistan, which makes it more prosperous than provinces further to its southeast. Farmers tend to earn less than a dollar a day, but Ghazni has more than 10,000 government employees, merchants, and businessmen who earn around ten dollars a day.

Ghazni's economy has historically relied on agriculture and related activities, and does not have a large urban center like those found in most Afghan provinces. Fifty-seven percent of households derive at least some income from agriculture. Ghazni City has historically been a transport and trading town due to its location between Kabul and Kandahar, and its proximity to Pakistan.

Ghazni ranks 14th of the 34 provinces in overall healthcare and education. According to the Ghazni PDP, in 2006 more than 75 percent of the population reported having occasional problems acquiring enough food. Roughly 25 percent were estimated to regularly receive less than the required amount of calories.

INFRASTRUCTURE

Lack of infrastructure is a constraint to communication, security, and economic and social development. The Kabul-Kandahar highway passes through three district centers (Qara Bagh, Muqur, and Gelan) as well as the provincial capital, but there are few other paved roads in the province. Some small bridges have been built across the Arghandab River, in Jaghori for example. Ghazni City has a small airport.

Education

Overall literacy in Ghazni is estimated to be 20-35 percent, with male and female literacy estimated to be 48 percent and 21 percent, respectively. Younger people, aged 15-24 have a slightly higher literacy rate, likely the result of schooling received in Iran or Pakistan. Literacy rates are higher in Hazara areas than in Pashtun ones. Hazaras favor schooling for both boys and girls because they see it as a way out of poverty. Literacy rates are especially low among the Kuchis (around one percent), which is not surprising given their nomadic existence. In recent years, Taliban pressure has forced the closure of many schools, in some cases by burning or damaging buildings. According to the UN, Jaghori district has the most schools in Ghazni, with 33 schools. The province has one university which was established in Ghazni City after 2002. It remains small and poorly supplied.

Healthcare

During the war years, as the government's healthcare system fell into dysfunction, healthcare was increasingly provided by NGOs, many of whom operated from Pakistan. Since 2002, the government has been relatively successful at rebuilding the healthcare system, mainly by focusing on the provision of a standard Ministry of Public Health (MoPH) Basic Package of Health Services to be available to all Afghans. In addition, the government contracted NGOs to deliver services. Ghazni is one of the 13 provinces whose health services are funded by USAID through the central MoPH. Ghazni has seen a steady improvement in the availability of healthcare, although insecurity has had a negative effect. The 2008 annual evaluation of national health system performance scored Ghazni 21st out of the 29 provinces for which data were available.

Electricity

Power is extremely limited in Ghazni. Twenty-five percent of households maintain their own generators, the highest percentage in the country. Some micro-hydro power generators were introduced under the National Solidarity Program (NSP) in Malistan, Nowar, and Jaghori. Improved with funds from the PRT, a power station in Ghazni City provides regular but limited power in the urban center. Privately owned generators can supplement this for AFS 45 ($1) per kW. The lack of power has limited the ability of farmers and traders to store perishable agricultural products and for entrepreneurs to develop small industry.

Transportation

The Kabul-Kandahar highway, which passes through the province and Ghazni City, is the most significant transportation project implemented in Afghanistan since 2001. It has reduced travel time from Kabul to Ghazni City to two hours, though travel from Ghazni to outlying districts can take several hours more on unpaved roads (these are slowly being improved – *see Ch. 5*). A range of private buses are offered in Ghazni City for locals who want to travel around the province or to Kabul or Kandahar. Between 2008 and 2009, the road to Ghazni was perceived to become somewhat safer. Transportation of goods remains complicated because of the risk of hijacking; large convoys use the road and appear to have made arrangements with local tribes and militias, sometimes allegedly paying the Taliban protection money.

Irrigation

Lack of water poses a major constraint to agriculture in the province. Even before the war, land was cultivated in some areas on a three-year rotation due to shortage of irrigation water. The war years saw a major degradation of existing facilities. Today, streams provide 44 percent of Ghazni's population with their irrigation water, conduits supply another 29 percent, and a smaller amount receive water from springs. The streams are frequently fed by karezes (underground systems of man-made canals that tap aquifers through underground tunnels which can extend for several miles before surfacing). Karezes are also a significant source of water on their own. However, the increasing use of tubewells is leading to a falling water table. Water resources in one area are drained by another area's tubewell. Water is accumulated in the province's three man-made reservoirs: Band-e Sardeh, Zanakhan, and Band-e Sultan. Nowar and Moqor Lakes are the two natural bodies of water within the province. Scarcity of water poses a serious threat to the long-term viability of settlements and may cause conflict in the future.

Telecommunications

The provincial center and surrounding areas are served by the three main mobile telephone companies: Roshan, AWCC, and Areeba. According to locals, Roshan gives the best coverage. In the mountainous areas of Jaghori district, for instance, its high transmitters make it the only viable network. However, this coverage is good only in the secure and more populated parts of the province; the less populated west and north have less coverage. In the eastern districts, the Taliban has intimidated companies into shutting down networks at night, or occasionally during the day, to prevent their movements being tracked. Afghans who do not have mobile phones can use call points which offer land lines for use for a fee. Even these are a long walk away for some.

KEY ECONOMIC SECTORS

In addition to agriculture, Ghazni's population is involved in activities such as shop keeping, working for NGOs, government service, and providing day labor. Formal sector employment is scarce and highly sought after. Remittances are a key source of livelihood for all ethnic groups in Ghazni – the province has the third highest percentage of rural households receiving remittances from family members working abroad.

Agriculture

Fifty-seven percent of Ghazni's households have agricultural income of some sort. Agriculture is a key sector. Unfortunately, the absence of water has led to a decrease in cultivated land. According to the Ministry of Agriculture, Irrigation, and Livestock, roughly six percent of cultivated land is rain-fed, although this varies greatly by district. Before the war, Ghazni exported wheat to Kabul and Kandahar.

Cereal crops (mainly wheat and rice) are grown on 59 percent of Ghazni's agricultural land, while orchards take up 23 percent, fruits 11 percent, and vegetables seven percent. The most important crops are wheat, barley, and maize. The main fruit and vegetable crops are grapes, apricots, apples, plums, beans, chick peas, potatoes, tomatoes, onions, cucumbers, pumpkins, watermelons, melons, leeks, peppers, almonds, and walnuts. The majority of grapes are converted to raisins, most of which are exported. During the 1960s and 1970s, Afghanistan supplied roughly 60 percent of the international market for raisins. Declining grape output, degradation of infrastructure for production and quality control, and the dissolution of international market linkages have ended Afghanistan's dominance in the raisin market. Apples and dried plums are exported to Pakistan, India, and the Gulf States. Many of the shops in Ghazni are involved in selling dry fruits. Apples are typically bought at the farm gate, and much of the packing, transport, and marketing is done by outsiders. Dairy products sold locally include *qerut* (dried yogurt), butter, and *chaka* (drained, thickened yogurt). Some fish are found in natural and man-made bodies of water.

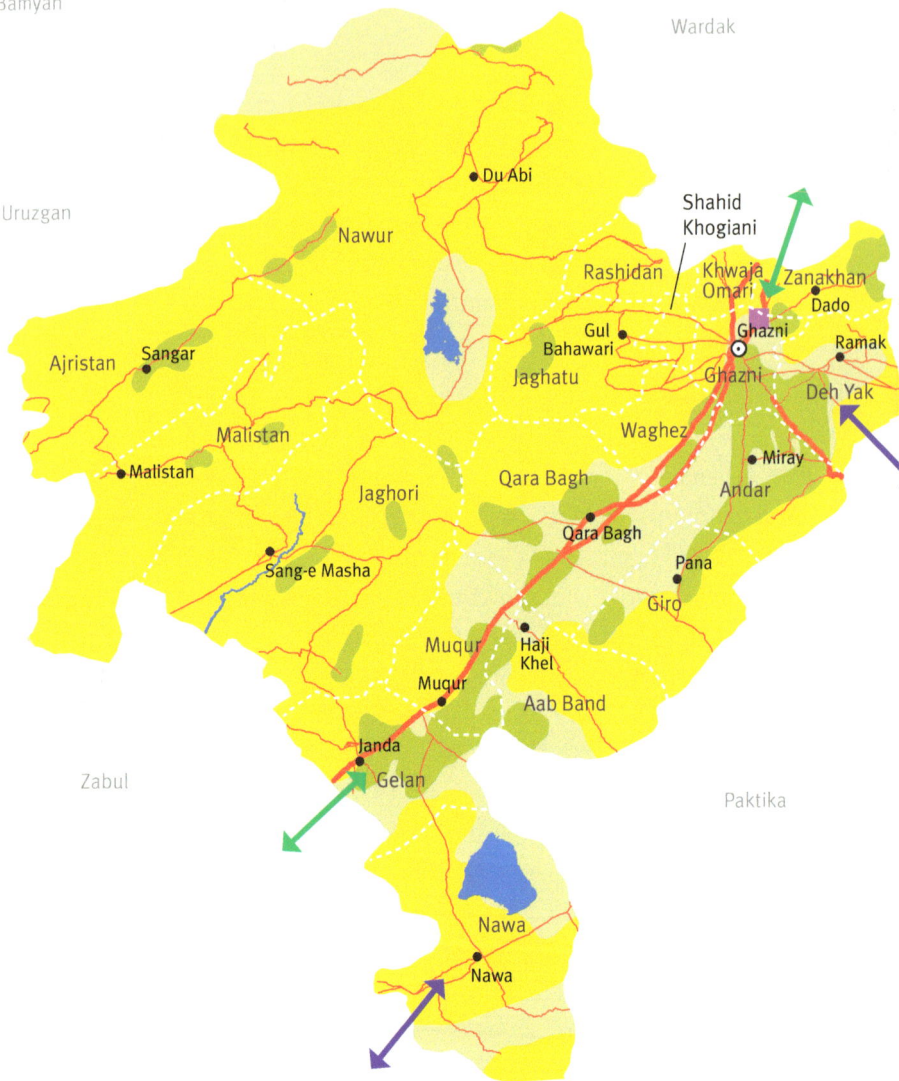

Map 3. Economic Map of Ghazni

Bamyan

Wardak

Du Abi

Uruzgan

Nawur

Shahid
Khogiani

Rashidan

Khwaja
Omari

Zanakhan

Dado

Gul
Bahawari

Ghazni

Ramak

Ghazni

Ajristan

Sangar

Jaghatu

Deh Yak

Malistan

Waghez

Malistan

Qara Bagh

Jaghori

Andar

Miray

Qara Bagh

Pana

Sang-e Masha

Giro

Muqur

Haji
Khel

Muqur

Aab Band

Janda

Zabul

Gelan

Paktika

Nawa

Nawa

Pakistan

Map 3. Economic Map of Ghazni

Roads		Arable Land
District Border		Range Land
River		Factory
Provincial Center		Trade Routes
City		Smuggling Routes

Over the last 30 years, agriculture has shifted from cereals to vegetables and orchards, partly in line with the government plans to encourage cash crops. Drought in the early 2000s and seasonal floods in 2006 drastically reduced the yields from all crops, and drought and conflict reduced livestock by as much as 70 percent. Starvation was reported in remote parts of Ghazni in the winter of 2006. However, crops flourished in 2009.

Like provinces further to the southeast, there is a high incidence of land ownership in Ghazni. Roughly half the population owns some amount of land, although the parcels may be extremely small and incapable of providing a household with a full livelihood. All but the largest landowners are involved in farming others' land and/or working off-farm. The most common arrangement is sharecropping, with the tenant receiving either a quarter or a third of the output and all inputs provided by the owner. Leasing of land is uncommon. Due to population pressure, land fragmentation, and off-farm income opportunities, the incidence of sharecropping has been reducing over time. It also seems clear that the average size of holdings has decreased over the last 30 years.

Trading and small enterprise

Other common livelihoods include wool production, *gelam* (carpet) and *namad* (felt) production, sheep skin processing, brick making, ironworking, and copper-smithing. Unfortunately, most of these industries have contracted in recent years due to many supply- and demand-side factors, including drought, lack of well-functioning markets, weak infrastructure, and the availability of imported products which are either cheaper or perceived to be more modern. Jaghori district has traditionally produced embroidery but this, too, has suffered. A small factory in Roza produces cheap pressure cookers for the local market, while there is at least one "factory" (a simple workshop) making sweets.

Many in Ghazni, particularly Hazaras, look to education as a path out of poverity for their families. Access to schools, such as this one, varies greatly across the districts of Ghazni.

PHOTO BY MICHAEL SMITH

Chapter 5
International Community and
Reconstruction Activities

The drafting of the Afghanistan National Development Strategy (ANDS) sought to allow Afghan stakeholders at provincial, district, and community levels to contribute to the planning process. As a part of this process, Ghazni developed a Provincial Development Plan (PDP) with input from the 18 District Development Assemblies (DDAs) District Development Plans. These documents are the coordinating documents for reconstruction and development at the provincial and district levels.

PROVINCIAL RECONSTRUCTION TEAM (PRT)

The PRT has existed in Ghazni since January 2004. It is now a joint US-Polish PRT with a US commander and US and Polish deputies.

The PRT is building roads to link district centers to the main highway. In September 2009 they completed such a road to Khwaja Omari district center. The PRT is also supplying medical equipment to local hospitals and clinics and making micro-grants to local businesses. The Ghazni PRT, as well as other PRTs throughout the country, constantly works to mentor district officials and community leaders.

Non-Governmental Organizations (NGOs)

NGOs have a limited presence in Ghazni, largely due to the inhospitable security situation.

OTHER INTERNATIONAL ACTORS & PROJECTS

In theory, the Ministry of Agriculture, Irrigation, and Livestock (MAIL) has 12 departments at the provincial level intended to provide a wide agricultural extension and support services including animal extensions, cooperatives, and beekeeping. In reality, the capacity to do so is almost non-existent. Assistance is being provided to the MAIL by FAO, DACAAR, CoAR, ADA, HAFO, and ICARDA. There are also a number of agricultural institutions, including cooperatives and seed growers associations with different levels of activity.

Microfinance programs have been introduced by BRAC, DACAAR, and Community Housing Foundation (CHF) in Ghazni and Khawaja Omri districts. In 2005, 38 percent of households reported taking out loans, most of which likely went to consumption; over half used their largest loan to buy food. As borrowing informally from relatives and neighbors may not be considered a "loan," the actual percentage of households which are in debt is likely much higher.

Table 5: International NGOs in Ghazni

AGENCY	ACTIVITY
Danish Committee for Afghanistan Relief (DACAAR)	NSP
CARE International	NSP and education
DAI/Local Governance Community Development	Local governance and community development
Swedish Committee for Afghanistan (SCA)	School construction and education materials
BRAC	Literacy courses
Norwegian Afghanistan Committee (NAC)	Education, health, and environment
Shelter Now International (SNI)	Humanitarian aid and housing
IbnSina	Health
Sanayee Development Organization (SDO)	Education
Bakhtar Development Foundation (BDF)	Health
Coordination of Afghanistan Relief (COAR)	Adult literacy
Helping Afghan Farmers Organizations (HAFO)	Water, women's literacy, and employment
Afghan Amputee Bicyclists for Rehabilitation and Recreation (AABRAR)	Mobility for amputees
Afghan Women Service and Education Organization (AWSE)	Women's employment, etc.
Afghanistan Development Association (ADA)	Health, education, and agriculture
Cooperation for Peace and Unity (CPAU)	Conflict analysis
International Medical Corps (IMC)	Health
Management Sciences for Health (Tech Serve) (MSH)	Health
Ockenden International (Ockenden)	Displaced persons
Ufuq (Horizon) Welfare Society (UWS)	Education
Ghazni Rural Support Program (GRSP)	Roads and rural development
Shuhada	Health, education, and income generation for women
Afghanistan Farm Service Alliance (AFSA)	Agriculture

A local radio station. Due to low literacy rates, radio is the most prevalent form of media in Ghazni, but rumors, spread by word of mouth, are often a more trusted source of information.

PHOTO BY MICHAEL SMITH

Chapter 6
Information and Influence

MEDIA ACTIVITY & INFLUENCE

Information sharing in Ghazni is limited by the low literacy rates. Therefore, the newspapers published irregularly in Ghazni, including the government weekly *Sanae*, *Arj*, *Zam Zam*, *Mehartaban*, and *Paiwand*, are not an important source of information. The state-owned and private television stations are a more popular source of information, but broadcast only about six hours per day with a range of 30 miles. Television stations primarily reach only those living in and around Ghazni City, and, of course, those who can afford a television and electricity.

Radio is by far the most popular source of information. In addition to the 24-hour state-owned Radio Afghanistan, Radio Ghaznawian (People of Ghazni) is the most popular radio station in the provincial capital. It receives USAID funds and is a member of the Internews Network, an international media development organization. Second and third most popular are Radio Omaid Jawan and Deh Kada, both privately owned. Jaghori and Malistan districts also have private radio stations. In August 2009, all three provincial radio stations were told by the Taliban to go off air; they were allowed to resume broadcasting only if they stopped all music and entertainment and avoided reporting on the presidential election campaigns. They complied.

The Taliban also has its own radio station, called Shariat Gagh (Voice of Islamic Law). It is received at least in the eastern districts. After an eight year hiatus following the removal of the Taliban in 2001, Shariat Gagh resumed broadcasting in July 2009.

INFORMATION SHARING AND NETWORKS

A high percentage of information is circulated outside of the formal media. Rumors spread quickly in Afghanistan, moving from one person to another, often mutating as they go. They are most popular when they conform to preconceived beliefs and do not need a factual basis to become widespread. One rumor that is widespread, for example, is that the US military has transported Taliban fighters to the north of Afghanistan in order to assist the insurgency. This rumor was started by an Afghan official and appeared to be endorsed by President Karzai at one point. It is essentially credible to some Afghans not only because it was started by an official, but because it explains why the insurgency in Afghanistan still survives and expands despite the massive international presence. Some such rumors may be started maliciously, others simply start from Afghans' heightened religious and political sensitivities.

Friday sermons at mosques are among the most powerful means of communication in Afghanistan. They are well-attended: it is an obligation for Sunnis to pray at the mosque on Fridays. The mullah who gives the sermon may well be the best-educated person in the community and because of this, in addition to his religious status, he is heard with respect. Sermons are usually religious in character but frequently make political points. They often pick up on current news stories and rumors and, by repeating them, make them more widely believed. The Ministry of Hajj and Islamic Affairs in Kabul claims that it pays prayer leaders at all mosques across the country, and tells them what to say in their sermons. In reality it is at most a small minority of mosques that receive government funding and guidance. Specifically in Ghazni, local sources say instead that the mosques are paid by and loyal to the jihadi movements Hezb-e Islami and Jamiat-e Islami, or else the Taliban. Religious schools (madrassas) for students training to become mullahs are very influential in determining the mullah's future political and theological attitudes.

The Disarmament, Demobilization, and Reintegration (DDR) Program has had mixed successes in Ghazni. While roughly 650 militants have been disarmed, the security situation remains poor. The Afghan National Police have frequently been used in counterterror efforts in the province, leading to high ANP fatality rates in the eastern part of Ghazni.

PHOTO BY MICHAEL SMITH

Chapter 7
The Big Issues

TALIBAN INFLUENCE

The Taliban's influence has grown in Pashtun areas over the past several years. Pashtuns have a complex relationship with the Taliban, especially in Ghazni where no tribe is openly hostile to the Taliban. While the Taliban's ultra-conservative ideology does not have wide appeal, they are seen as less corrupt than the government and more capable of delivering services, for example justice. Ghazni Pashtun men (and even women) do not see the Taliban as their enemy. Indeed, their family members may be members of the Taliban. Many are afraid of the consequences of disobeying the Taliban, and do not see it as worth the risk. Hazara areas, by contrast, are relatively free of Taliban activity. Hazaras see the Taliban as their enemy. While a few of them collaborated with the Taliban in the 1990s, this was done only once all resistance appeared to have failed.

The Taliban is a loosely-organized movement. In Ghazni, many of their members are from the province itself. Some are outsiders, sent in by the national leadership to stiffen the resolve of local members. The national leadership, including the Peshawar and Quetta shuras, only occasionally issues instructions to all their followers as they continue to try to institute an organized shadow government. Nevertheless, most Taliban activity is planned and executed locally. High-profile attacks are more of an exception, such as the complex terrorist attack in Kabul that killed numerous foreigners in October 2008. These are likely planned by senior leaders of one insurgent movement or another. There have been few of these attacks in Ghazni.

MOTIVES OF INSURGENT GROUPS

The motives of these groups vary widely, and include ideology (fundamentalist Islam), nationalism (anti-foreigners), the attainment of personal power/wealth, the protection of local tribal powerbases, and the larger goal of regaining political power from the government. Some are inspired by religious education they received at madrassas that taught a radical form of Islam (the Ghazni madrassa, for example, has Taliban sympathies). Some elements may desire to preserve space for illicit activities, including the trafficking of narcotics.

Insurgent groups exploit a dearth of education, the lack of government information, and the lack of economic opportunities in Ghazni's communities, particularly for impressionable youth. Fear and resistance to outsiders, the piety of the population, and tribal/cultural connections to insurgent members all serve to allow vulnerable populations to be manipulated into support or recruitment. In Ghazni, insurgents have mainly succeeded in gaining control of rural areas by intimidating and assassinating government officials and local leaders. Violence occurs when they are confronted; an absence of violence in the remote areas (such as in Nawa district) does not prove an absence of Taliban.

ETHNIC TENSION

Ethnic tensions in Afghanistan have been prevalent for centuries. Pashtuns, Tajiks, and Hazaras all have certain grievances against each other. Afghanistan was traditionally ruled by Pashtuns, with Hazaras and Tajiks treated as secondary citizens. Only after the Communist revolution in 1978 did ethnic tensions become violent. The Afghan civil war that followed the collapse of the Communist government was bloody, pitting the ethnic groups against each other. The Taliban discriminated against Hazaras and, to some extent, against Tajiks as well. After the Taliban fell, Tajiks dominated the state security forces and some Pashtuns saw the hunting down of former Talibs as evidence of discrimination. Indeed, Pashtuns perceive themselves as deprived of power since the Taliban were overthrown. In Ghazni specific disputes over land rights have created further Pashtun-Hazara tensions. All these different phases of the country's history have left a legacy of mistrust.

Ethnic tensions can make co-operation in government difficult. For example, the Ghazni Provincial Council was deadlocked by arguments between Pashtuns and Hazaras over who should lead the PC. Ethnic rivalries also make it difficult for the Taliban to recruit Tajiks and Hazaras. At the same time, it is difficult for Hazara and Tajik security officials to gain the full co-operation of Pashtun colleagues and civilians. Remarkably, Dr. Shah Jan, head of the Ghazni NDS, appears to have gained the cooperation of Pashtun colleagues despite being a Hazara.

Map 4. Conflict Map of Ghazni

Bamyan

Wardak

Uruzgan

Du Abi

Nawur

Shahid
Khogiani

Rashidan

Khwaja
Omari

Zanakhan
Dado

Ajristan

Sangar

Gul
Bahawari

Ghazni

Ramak

Malistan

Jaghatu

Deh Yak

Malistan

Waghez

Miray

Qara Bagh

Andar

Jaghori

Qara Bagh

Pana

Sang-e Masha

Giro

Muqur

Haji
Khel

Muqur

Aab Band

Janda

Zabul

Gelan

Paktika

Nawa

Nawa

Pakistan

Legend:

- Roads
- District Border
- River
- ⊙ Provincial Center
- • City
- HIG
- Haqqani Network
- Taliban
- ↔ Transit Routes

CHANGING ALLEGIANCES

Over the course of more than thirty years of conflict, Afghans have learned to ignore ideological differences, at least to some extent, and ally themselves with the winning side in a conflict. The pro-government elements in Ghazni include former communists, former pro-Iran Islamists, and some fairly extreme Sunni Muslim fundamentalists. They fought each other in the 1980s and 1990s but now are allied and are mostly supportive of Coalition forces. The Taliban and other anti-government fighters are ideologically more united, but they too sometimes draw in people who essentially are fighting the government because of personal or tribal disputes with government officials. Tribal solidarity is less obvious than in other southeastern provinces (Paktika, Paktya, and Khost), but it still plays a role in people's behavior.

Iron-working and copper-smithing are traditional Ghaznian livelihoods. Blacksmiths' shops such as this one are important for the 90% of Ghaznians who live in small villages or on isolated farmsteads.

PHOTO BY MICHAEL SMITH

APPENDICES

TIMELINE OF KEY EVENTS

625: Alp Tigin, an ethnic Turk, takes control of land around modern-day Ghazni. Thus begins the Ghaznawi dynasty which eventually rules a territory that includes most of modern Afghanistan, Iran, and Pakistan.

1152: The Ghorids sack and destroy Ghazni City.

1186: The Ghorids defeat the Ghaznawis, ending their dynasty.

1221: Genghis Khan's armies devastate Ghazni as part of their conquest of Central Asia.

1747: Ahmad Shah Baba becomes king of the Abdali (Durrani) tribe and conquers Ghazni, bringing it into modern-day Afghanistan.

1839: The British Army conquers and briefly occupies Ghazni City.

1979-1992: Fighting between communists and mujahedin causes widespread suffering and emigration.

2002: Asadullah Khalid becomes Ghazni's first governor.

2005: Khalid is replaced by Sher Alam. The assassination of government officials reaches its peak.

2006: Merajuddin Pathan replaces Sher Alam. Murders and kidnappings remain frequent.

2007: 23 Korean Christians are kidnapped in Ghazni along the Kabul-Kandahar highway; two are killed; others are released for ransom. Faizanullah Faizan becomes governor, achieves temporary reduction in violence.

2008: Sher Khosti is appointed as governor but is then quickly replaced by Osman Osmani, the present governor.

COMMON COMPLIMENTS OF ISAF FORCES

- Compliments, and complaints, should be accepted politely but evaluated carefully. Compliments in particular are often used as ways of winning favor.

- Afghans will often compliment the United States as a country. They may say that the US is more sensitive, has more friendly citizens, or that it is stronger than another country. These compliments are either meant sincerely or out of politeness.

- Afghans praise the US and ISAF forces for removing the Taliban and installing a democratic government. Many Afghans, including Pashtuns, mean this sincerely. A few may not.

- Afghans will praise ISAF troops for removing warlords, or for a stand taken against warlords. This sentiment stems from the resentment many Afghans feel towards the Mujahedin for their conduct during the early 1990s. It is also equally likely that some Afghans may be critical of the warlords' removal.

- Afghans praise the funding of projects funded by donor countries. However, complaints tend to outweigh praise, especially as some large-scale projects do not bring direct and immediate benefits to poorer Afghans.

- Individuals who have managed to build genuine personal relationships with locals earn the greatest respect and compliments among Afghans. Personal loyalties are strong among Afghans, but they take time to develop. Individual Afghans who feel they have been helped by a particular ISAF government or institution may well feel a certain loyalty to it. However, this loyalty depends on how well the subsequent relationship has been maintained.

COMMON COMPLAINTS OF ISAF FORCES

- Afghans are critical of airstrikes that kill civilians.

- Afghans are displeased by house searches because they find them demeaning and an offense to Islamic sensibilities.

- Afghans see the lack of coordination between ISAF and the Afghan army/police, along with the continued strength of the Taliban, as indications that foreign forces have their own separate agenda and do not want peace.

- Afghans think that the international community talks to warlords and drug dealers, which proves to them that ISAF is not interested in establishing the rule of law.

- Pashtuns believe Tajiks and Hazaras have more power now than Pashtuns because the international community is anti-Pashtun. Non-Pashtuns, likewise, believe the international community is pro-Pashtun and is failing to allow equal rights for their ethnic group.

- Some locals believe that ISAF/Afghan government negotiations with the Taliban are proof that the international community is seeking to restore the Taliban to power in Afghanistan.

- Some Afghans believe foreigners are in Afghanistan for their own interests.

- Many Afghans opposed to Karzai felt betrayed by the ambiguous results of the August 2009 Presidential Election. They believe voters took great risks by voting in the elections and were betrayed because the international community allowed a great deal of fraud. ISAF nations should have helped make it a better process. Supporters of Karzai alternately believe foreigners interfered to try to weaken President Karzai.

FAUX PAS TO AVOID

- Avoid appearing to side with Pakistan or Iran. One visiting dignitary once said to a group of Afghans that Afghanistan was important to his country "because of Pakistan" (meaning that Pakistan was more of a strategic threat). This phrase could be found insulting.

- Do not make any reference to the female members of a Pashtun family.

- A man should not touch an Afghan woman – even to shake her hand, unless she extends hers first. Touching your hand to your heart is often acceptable as an alternative; or nothing at all.

- Do not intrude on the privacy of a family, particularly its female members, except in cases of dire need. In some families the women are never seen by strangers, in others they need first to veil themselves.

- Dogs are unclean according to Islam, and many Afghans will feel they cannot pray in a place where a dog has been. Therefore, the use of dogs in house searches is very much disliked.

DAY IN THE LIFE OF A RURAL GHAZNIAN

The most important daily ritual for Afghans is the five prayers (Shia prey three times a day and Sunnis prey five times a day, generally). The time of the prayers fluctuates with the season. For instance, the first and last prayers are taken during sunrise and sunset. At four in the morning, the family wakes and washes and prepares for the first prayer of the day at dawn. They then sit down for breakfast, usually based around bread and tea. The men head to the field to work around five o'clock and finish around eleven. The family gathers at home for midday prayers and lunch, their main meal of the day. After lunch, they rest and digest.

DAY IN THE LIFE OF AN URBAN GHAZNIAN

Even for urban Ghaznians, the most important daily ritual remains the three/five prayers. The time of the prayers fluctuates with the season – for instance, the first and last prayers are taken during sunrise and sunset. At four in the morning, people begin to wake, wash and prepare for the day. People eat breakfast, usually based around bread and tea. Men who work for the government head to the office around eight o'clock. Shopkeepers and businessmen may go to work earlier. Families gather at home for midday prayers and lunch, their main meal of the day. After afternoon prayer, generally around four o'clock depending upon the season, government offices close; shops stay open later. Dinner is held after evening prayer.

List of Key Contacts

Governor	Dr. Mohammad Osman Osmani	0799-547-200 0799-600-474 0700-306-694
Governor Secretary	Alishah	0799-566-175
Deputy Governor	Mohammad Kazem Allahyar	0799-231-166
CoP	Gen. Khial Baz Sherzai	0799-020-947 0700-788-807
Deputy CoP	Abdurrahman	0799-274-444 0777-382-638
NDS Head	Dr. Shah Jan	0796-544-223
NDS Deputy	General Samar	0799-131-461 0774-179-926 0786-947-750
ANA Batallion Commander	General Rajab Ali Rashid	0700-263-431

FURTHER READING AND SOURCES

Books

- Ahmed Rashid, *Taliban: Militant Islam, Oil, and Fundamentalism in Central Asia*, 2001

- Ahmed Rashid, *Descent into Chaos: The US and the Disaster in Pakistan, Afghanistan, and Central Asia*, New York: Penguin Group, 2008.

- Barnett Rubin, *The Fragmentation of Afghanistan*, 2001

- Barnett Rubin, *Afghanistan's Uncertain Transition from Turmoil to Normalcy*, 2007

- Ben Macintyre, *The Man Who Would Be King: The First American in Afghanistan*, New York: Farrar, Straus, and Giroux, 2005.

- Greg Mortenson, *Three Cups of Tea: One Man's Mission to Promote Peace... One School at a Time,* 2007. (Excellent understanding of how to succeed with the people and culture)

- Larry Goodson, *Afghanistan's Endless War: State Failure, Regional Politics, and the Rise of the Taliban*, 2001.

- Louis Dupree, *Afghanistan*, Princeton: Princeton University Press, 1979.

- Michael Griffin, *Reaping the Whirlwind: The Taliban Movement in Afghanistan*, London: Pluto Press, 2001.

- Sarah Chayes, *The Punishment of Virtue: Inside Afghanistan After the Taliban*, New York: Penguin Group, 2007.

- Steve Coll, *Ghost Wars: The Secret History of the CIA, Afghanistan, and Bin Laden, From the Soviet Invasion to September 10, 2001*, New York Penguin Press, 2004

- *ISAF PRT Handbook*, 4th Ed. 2009. NATO.

- Olaf Caroe, *The Pathans: 550 B.C. – A.D. 1957*, New York: St. Martins Press, 1959.

Articles

- President Karzai. "The Afghanistan National Development Strategy." 2006. *www.reliefweb.int/rw/RWFiles2006.nsf/ FilesByRWDocUNIDFileName/KHII-6LK3R2-unama-afg-30jan2. pdf/$File/unama-afg-30jan2.pdf*

- Afghanistan Research and Evaluation Unit. "Elections in 2009 and 2010: Technical and Contextual Challenges to Building Democracy in Afghanistan." November 2008. *www.areu.org. af/index.php?option=com_docman&Itemid=26&task=doc_ download&gid=612*

- G.H. Orris and J.D. Bliss. "Mines and Mineral Occurrences of Afghanistan – Open Report 02-110." US Geological Survey, US Department of the Interior, 2002.

Websites

- Afghanistan Research and Evaluation Unit (publishes the Afghanistan A to Z guide), *www.areu.org.af/index. php?option=com_frontpage&Itemid=25*

- Afghanistan Information Management Services, *www.aims.org.af/*

- Afghanistan Online (Links to Official IRA and embassy websites), *www.afghan-web.com/politics/*

- Naval Postgraduate School Program for Culture and Conflict Studies, *www.nps.edu/Programs/CCS/index.html*

- USAID, *www.usaid.gov/locations/asia/countries/afghanistan/*

Bibliography

- GRM International, *Regional Rural Economic Regeneration Strategies (RRERS)*, 2006.

- UNIDATA, *Ghazni Province: A Socio-Economic Profile*, 1992.

- The Islamic Republic of Afghanistan, *Estimated Population of Afghanistan 2008 – 2009*, Central Statistics Office, 1387 (2008).

- US Naval Postgraduate College Program for Culture and Conflict Studies, *Executive Summary*, 2008.

- Ministry of Rural Rehabilitation and Development, *Provincial Development Plans, Ghazni Provincial Profile*, 2008.

- Ludwig W. Adamec, "Dictionary of Afghan Wars, Revolutions, and Insurgencies," *Historical Dictionaries of Wars, Revolution, and Civil Unrest*, No. 1, Lanham, MD and London: Scarecrow Press, 1996.

- Niamatullah Ibrahimi, "Divide and Rule: State Penetration in Hazarajat (Afghanistan) From the Monarchy to the Taliban," *Crisis States Working Papers Series*, No.2, Working Paper 42, January 2009.

- Alessandro Monsutti, "The Impact of War on Social, Political and Economic Organisation in Southern Hazarajat" M.R. Djalili, A. Monsutti, and A. Neubauer (eds), *Le monde turco-iranien en question*, 2008.

- Gilles Dorronsoro, *Revolution Unending: Afghanistan, 1979 to the Present*, translated from the French by John King, New York: Columbia University Press in association with the Centre d'Etudes et de Recherches Internationales, Paris, c2005.

- Antonio Giustozzi, *Koran, Kalashnikov, and Laptop: The Neo-Taliban Insurgency in Afghanistan*, New York: Columbia University Press, c2008.

- Central Statistics Office, The Islamic Republic of Afghanistan (with assistance of UNFPA); *Ghazni: A Socio-Economic and Demographic Profile*; 2003.

- Ministry of Rural Rehabilitation and Development and Central Statistics Office, The Islamic Republic of Afghanistan, *The National Risk and Vulnerability Assessment 2005*, June 2007.

- The Islamic Republic of Afghanistan and UNICEF, *Best Estimates of Social Indicators for Children in Afghanistan 1990-2005*, May 2006.

- The Islamic Republic of Afghanistan and UNICEF, *Best Estimates Provincial Fact Sheet 8: Ghazni*, undated.

- Afghanistan Research and Evaluation Unit, *A to Z Guide to Afghanistan Assistance 2009* (seventh edition), January 2009.

- United Nations Assistance Mission in Afghanistan (UNAMA), *Humanitarian Provincial Profiles*, 2008.

www.ingramcontent.com/pod-product-compliance
Lightning Source LLC
Chambersburg PA
CBHW040128270326
41927CB00001B/26